CW00420624

Ann + Nick

PRAYING IN THE
IGNATIAN SPIRIT

GERALD O'MAHONY S.J.

Kevin
Mayhew

First published in 1998 by
KEVIN MAYHEW LTD
Rattlesden
Bury St Edmunds
Suffolk IP30 0SZ

ISBN 1 84003 155 7
Catalogue No 1500172

Front cover
Hands of an Apostle, 1508
(brush drawing) by Albrecht Durer (1471-1528).
Graphische Sammlung Albertina, Vienna/Bridgeman
Art Library, London/New York.

Background: *Poppies* by Alan Bedding

Cover design by Angela Staley
Series editor: Robert B. Kelly
Typesetting by Louise Selfe
Printed and bound in Great Britain

INTRODUCTION

Saint Ignatius was born in 1491 and died in 1556. He was a Basque and spent his young manhood as a retainer to a Spanish duke, serving his liege lord as required, as courtier, or soldier. By his own account he was an unruly character, but deep within was the desire to be a knight in shining armour, doing great deeds for his noble master and for the favour of the noble lady he admired. The age of shining knights was long past even then – but that was the way Ignatius' dream went.

He was stopped in his tracks by a cannon ball crushing his knee in battle at Pamplona. During his convalescence he had a conversion of heart: still the same Ignatius, but Jesus was his master, and Mary the noble lady whose favour he sought. Ignatius himself reckoned that, in the months and years that followed, it was God himself who taught him to pray.

Soon this wholehearted convert was teaching others to pray as God had taught him. The Inquisition soon stopped him, imprisoned him even, for teaching religion without being properly qualified. So at the age of 33, Ignatius went back to school; then on to a Spanish university to study philosophy; to the Sorbonne in Paris to study theology; then to Italy to be ordained priest. By this time he had a group of followers, 'companions', who became the nucleus of a new religious order, the Society of Jesus – or the Jesuits, as they came to be known.

Ignatius himself recorded his experience of being taught to pray by God in a small book called **The Spiritual Exercises**, which provides the inspiration for this present, much smaller book. Sometimes it follows the letter of **The Spiritual Exercises**, with direct quotes; always it follows its spirit. They are seldom 'written prayers to pray'. Most often they are 'exercises', suggesting how to get ready to pray, ways to pray and what to pray about – but always expecting the person praying to use his or her own words and feelings.

As the centuries have gone by, many, many others have expressed their praying in their own words, in their own style. This collection offers a glimpse of some of these prayers, songs and poems: some old, some new; all reflecting the spirit of Ignatius.

Acknowledgements

My translations and adaptations
of **The Spiritual Exercises** are taken from
the *Versio Litteralis* of 1548,
approved by Pope Paul III.

My translation from the Gospels
and from Ignatius of Antioch
is from the original Greek.

My translation of the three prayers
and part of one Preface from the *Roman Missal*
is from the original Latin.

My translation of *Anima Christi* and
the excerpt from *De Imitatione Christi*
is from the original Latin.

For English translations of Ignatius' letters
I wish to thank the publishers of
Saint Ignatius Loyola: Letters to Women
by Hugo Rahner, 1960 Herder/Nelson,
now out of print.

The quotation from Mary Ward is from
Mary Ward, a world in contemplation
by Henriette Peters, translated by Helen Butterworth,
1994 Gracewing/Fowler Wright, Leominster,
used with permission.

My thanks to Tom McGuinness for permission
to reprint the lyrics of *All will be well in the end*
(© 1989 Tom McGuinness S.J.).

My thanks to John W. Padberg S.J.
and the Institute of Jesuit Sources, St Louis,
MO 63108, for permission to use the
'Prayer of an Ageing Jesuit';

and also to:
Paula Terroni F.C.J.
Kathleen Mulryan I.B.V.M.
Teresa House and Rita MacManus
Brian Grogan S.J.
Herbert Alonso S.J.
for help and/or permission to use
their words or their ideas;

and to Robert Kelly
for his patient promptings.

Some people long for heroics
    and get them.
Most people do not look for heroics
    but get them anyway.
This collection
    is for both kinds of people.

ANIMA CHRISTI

*This prayer was clearly one of Ignatius' favourites, because he uses it and refers to it extensively in **The Spiritual Exercises**.*

Life of Christ, make me holy;
    presence of Christ, heal me;
    chalice of Christ, intoxicate me;
    fountain of living water, spring up in me.

Passion of Christ, strengthen me;
    good Jesus, hear me;
    with your wounds, touch my heart;
    never let me be separated from you.

From your enemy, defend me;
    every moment that I die, call me,
    and bid me come to you
    that with the saints I may praise you
    for ever and ever.
Amen.

Unknown, probably 14th century
Trans. Gerald O'Mahony S.J.

THE GOOD NEWS

God from heaven speaks to Jesus:
   'You are my beloved son;
   I am well pleased with you.' *(Mark 1:11)*

Jesus passes the News to us
   and gives us the courage to say to God:

   'I am your beloved daughter;
   you are well pleased with me
      not because I am a good daughter,
        but because I am your daughter.

   'I am your beloved son;
   you are well pleased with me
      not because I am a good son,
        but because I am your son.'

Gerald O'Mahony S.J.

Two Simple Ways of Praying

1. Use the words of any famous or favourite prayer, any famous or favourite hymn. Ask yourself, 'To whom is this prayer addressed?', and put yourself in the presence of that person. Say the words very slowly, phrase by phrase, or even word by word. Do not let yourself go on to the next word or phrase until you have squeezed all the possible meaning and flavour out of the present one. If you are deeply struck by any particular word or phrase, stay there; do not worry about going on to finish all the words.

2. Another way to use famous or favourite prayers or hymns is to say the words slowly, one fresh word for each breath breathed out. No need to go back and repeat a word if the meaning escaped you or if you were distracted. The effects of this kind of praying are long-term: prayers prayed in this way tend to come to mind later, unbidden, at a time when they will help us.

*Based on **The Spiritual Exercises**, 249-260*

DEEP FOUNDATION

Human beings are created to receive their heavenly inheritance as a free gift from God, and then to thank God by praise, reverence and grateful service.

Everything else upon the face of the earth was created for the benefit of human beings, to help us become what we are made to be.

It follows, then, that we should use things only in so far as they help us toward our goal; similarly, we ought to avoid them in so far as they block our way toward that goal.

So we need to make ourselves free as regards all things created, wherever such a choice is possible and allowable. Consequently we will not wish for health rather than sickness, nor prefer riches to poverty, honours to being despised, and so on . . . rather we will desire and choose, according to circumstances, whichever leads us closer to the end for which we were created.

*Based on **The Spiritual Exercises**,*
23, 94, 170, 234

GRATITUDE (1)

How well-loved and honoured
   in heaven and on earth
   is gratitude,
   gratitude for all the blessings
   and gifts we have received.
Ingratitude, though,
   is the foundation,
   origin and source
   of all sins and of all evil.

From a letter by Ignatius (1555)

GRATITUDE (2)

What do you think, my soul, of the mercy of our Lord, so wide, unfailing, pure and infinite? He has need of nothing that we can give, yet out of the abundance of his love he is so full of care for his servants, as if all his happiness depended on them! What thanks, then, will you offer him? What can you ever do that would express full and proper thanks for such great mercy?

Try as best you can to please him. Scripture says, 'Be merciful, as your heavenly Father is merciful'. Try all you can then, not only to have compassion for your fellow-servants, but to have for them that pure affection with which the Father has compassion on us.

Robert Bellarmine S.J. (1542-1621)

GRATITUDE (3)

The following prayer now appears in our modern **Roman Missal** *as the Prayer after Communion for the 1st Sunday in Ordinary Time. The version below is a free translation from the Latin that Ignatius would have known and used in his time.*

> We call on your kindness,
> > most powerful God:
> > as you refresh us with your sacraments,
> > may we in turn be strengthened
> > to serve you worthily
> > living lives pleasing to you.

From the **Roman Missal**

GREAT DESIRES (1)

Whoever takes up these prayer exercises
   will be helped in a wonderful way
   if they enter into them
   with greatness of heart
   and total trust
   towards their Creator and Lord.

Let them offer to the divine Majesty
   every wish, and all their freedom,
   both as regards themselves
   and as regards everything they possess,
   so that their lives may be arranged
   according to God's most holy will.

The Spiritual Exercises, 5

GREAT DESIRES (2)

The following prayer now appears in our modern **Roman Missal** *as the Opening Prayer for the 27th Sunday in Ordinary Time. The version below is a literal translation from the Latin that Ignatius would have known and used in his time.*

> All-powerful, ever-living God,
>> in your abundant love for your children
>> you give us more than we deserve
>> and more than we ask for:
>> grant us your mercy in great measure;
>> forgive us when we have gone against
>>> our conscience,
>> and give us in addition
>> what we dare not even pray for.

> *From the* **Roman Missal**

Ignatius daydreamed of being a perfect knight, fulfilling the wishes of his beloved King, no matter how difficult the errand. He adopted as his motto 'For the greater glory of God', and sought to live it out by always choosing whatever gave more importance to God.

God is Love *(1 John 4:16)*; Love is never boastful *(1 Corinthians 13:4)*. Ignatius would set the record right!

Each of us, with our own background story, can choose our own motto – and it need have nothing to do with knights or kings, or warfare with swords, lances and flags. Warfare will exist in our lives; it cannot be avoided. But each of us can approach it from our own personal angle, in the way we feel called by God.

Choosing a motto

- supposing you had to design your personal coat of arms, what sort of phrase would you choose as your motto?

- make as wide a selection as possible of short phrases that appeal to you, from Scripture, from poems or other literature, from speeches, from significant things that people have said to you, that stick in your memory. If it is a long text, perhaps you can pick out a key phrase which sums up what is important in the text, and which reminds you of the rest.

- supposing you can take only eight of these phrases with you through life: which would you choose?

- and if you were only allowed three, which three would you feel you had to keep?

- then if you were allowed no more than one, which one would it have to be?

- don't be over-serious about this exercise! If tomorrow your choice seems wrong, then choose another that you are happy to stay with for some time.

- review your choice of motto every year or so.

- use your motto to help you in making a daily 'particular review' *(see pages 20, 21).*

As Kingfishers Catch Fire

As kingfishers catch fire, dragonflies draw flame;
   As tumbled over rim in roundy wells
   Stones ring; like each tucked string tells, each
      hung bell's
Bow swung finds tongue to fling out broad its name;
Each mortal thing does one thing and the same.
   Deals out that being indoors each one dwells;
   Selves – goes itself; **myself** it speaks and spells,
Crying **Whát I dó is me: for that I came.**

I say móre: the just man justices;
   Keeps gráce: that keeps all his goings graces;
Acts in God's eye what in God's eye he is –
   Christ. For Christ plays in ten thousand places,
Lovely in limbs, and lovely in eyes not his
   To the Father through the features of men's faces.

Gerard Manley Hopkins S.J. (1844-1889)

PARTICULAR REVIEW

Accentuate the positive

- every day, first thing in the morning, I try to recall my personal vocation, as expressed in my own personal motto. Let it draw me; pray that I live up to my motto in the day ahead.

- similarly, in the middle of the day, I try to recall my motto, and so revive my motivation. Having chosen a motto that I really want to keep, that is dear to my heart, recalling it never becomes boring.

- last thing at night I recall my personal calling, always glad to remember that God thinks more of my desires than of my performance.

Eliminate the negative

- I can use the same three moments in each day to pursue a particular fault in myself that I want to be free from. The night-time moment is most important, when I look back and count how many times that day I have given in to the fault.

- if I simply wish I were better, nothing much will change. Whereas, if I look with total honesty at the number of times I do some objectionable thing, then the number of times will drop. It usually does, gradually, and even completely, in the end.

Based on **The Spiritual Exercises**, *24-31*

GENERAL REVIEW

Not an examination of conscience, exactly, but a review of the day – or of the year, or of a lifetime – looking at it along with God.

- I become aware again of the presence of God, for example:

    'My God, here I am,
       here we are,
       you and I.
    No one else in the world
       can see exactly the scene
       my eyes are looking at
       at this moment;
       no one except you and I.
    All day long
       there has been this world within me,
       where we have shared everything.'

- I make a prayer to God, asking to see the most significant moments of the day.

- I let the day (or year, or whatever) unfold in my imagination, not seeking out anything in particular, but letting the times that meant most rise to the surface naturally, of their own accord. For the happy times, I give thanks; for sad or disappointing times, I ask comfort or forgiveness. From successes and failures, I learn the lesson for the future, filing it away in my memory for the next time something similar occurs.

- In all that happened, God was there with me; in spite of all, God loves me as much at the end of the day as at the beginning. I marvel at this and give thanks.

- I ask for the gift of being aware of the presence of God in my life tomorrow, not just at the end of the day, but as the day goes on.

*Based on **The Spiritual Exercises**, 32-44*

Colloquial Prayer

Colloquial prayer
    means praying the way
    one friend might speak to another;
    or as a servant might
    to the master or mistress.

This might be to ask for some grace;
    another time to ask forgiveness
    for some wrong we have done;
    another time simply
    to share thoughts, doubts, plans,
    the way we are feeling, and so on,
    and asking advice about them.

At the end, pray the 'Our Father'.

The Spiritual Exercises, 54

Threefold Conversation

Ignatius suggests this method to pray for important gifts or grace we think we need in order to be helpful to others.

1. I have a conversation with Mary.
   I tell her what it is I want to ask for.
   Will she help me?
   Will she come with me to Jesus,
      and ask him with me?
   I pray the 'Hail, Mary'.

2. I go with Mary to Jesus.
   I have a conversation with him about
      what it is I want.
   Will he help me?
   Will he come with Mary and me
      to the Father and ask him?
   I pray the *'Anima Christi'*.

3. I go with Jesus and Mary to the Father.
   I tell him what I want.
   I ask for it if it be his will
   or for something better if not what I ask.
   I pray the 'Our Father'.

See **The Spiritual Exercises**, *63 et al*

How and Where to Pray (1)

In following **The Spiritual Exercises**, Ignatius would want me to start by thinking about whatever is the concern of my prayer, and then to pass fairly quickly to conversing with God (or whoever it is to whom I am praying), expressing my feelings and my desires. The conversation part should be made with due reverence for the person to whom I am addressing the prayer.

I can pray kneeling, lying face down on the ground, sitting down, standing up . . . quite simply whichever helps to gain the grace for which I am asking.

*Compare **The Spiritual Exercises**, 3 and 76*

How and Where to Pray (2)

When you go to the door,
   imagine that it is God
   who wants to come in,
   and receive the person accordingly.

When the visitor is leaving,
   imagine that you are opening
   the door for God,
   not a human person;

this is the frame of mind to have,
   the signs of love and humility to show
   as you take leave of the visitor
   and let him out.

Alphonsus Rodrigues S.J. (1533-1617)

This is verity,
   to do what we have to do well.
Many think it nothing
   to do ordinary things.
But for us it is:
   to do ordinary things well.

Mary Ward (1585-1645)
Foundress of the Institute of the Blessed Virgin Mary

'To Know . . . and to Do'

Ignatius left over 7,000 letters; he frequently ended them like this:

. . . I close by asking God through his infinite goodness to give us the perfect grace to know his most holy will and to fulfil it completely.

(1536)

. . . I say no more except to commend myself to your prayers and to beg God our Lord to grant us the grace always to know his most holy will and to fulfil it completely.

(1554)

'IGNATIUS'

Saint Ignatius, second-century bishop of Antioch, was martyred in Rome around the year 110. It was in honour of this saint that Ignatius of Loyola changed his name from 'Inigo' to 'Ignatius'.

'. . . but be firmly convinced about the Nativity and the Passion and the Resurrection that took place in the time of Pontius Pilate's governorship. These things were done most truly and definitely by Jesus Christ, your hope. May none of you ever be diverted from that hope.'

Ignatius of Antioch, **Letter to the Magnesians***, 11*

'My love for all temporary things has been crucified. There is in me no fire of desire for those, but rather a brook of living water, murmuring *(literally, chattering)* within me and saying: "Come with me to the Father".'

Ignatius of Antioch, **Letter to the Romans***, 7*

THE MISSION OF JESUS

The Spirit of the Lord is upon me
   because he has anointed me
   to bring good news to the poor.
He has sent me to proclaim release to the captives
   and recovery of sight to the blind,
   to let the oppressed go free,
   to proclaim the year of the Lord's favour.

Luke 4:18, 19

FORGIVENESS OF ENEMIES

If these my offers be refused, and my endeavours
can take no place, and I, having run thousands of
miles to do you good, shall be rewarded with rigour,
I have no more to say but to commend your case
and mine to Almightie God, the Searcher of hearts,
who send us his grace, and set us at accord
before the day of payment, to the end we may at
last be friends in heaven, when all injuries shall
be forgotten.

Edmund Campion S.J. (1540-1581)
open letter to the Privy Council of Elizabeth I,
who later had him executed

To love the poor,
persever in the same,
live, die and Rise with
them was all the ayme
of
Mary Ward, who
having lived 60 years
and 8 days dyed
the 20th Jan. 1645

*Inscription on the tomb at Osbaldwick
of Mary Ward,
foundress of the Institute of the Blessed Virgin Mary*

THE COMING OF THE KING

First, remember what happened:
    how our Lady,
    already nine months pregnant,
    came from Nazareth, seated on a donkey,
    accompanied by Joseph
    and,
    we may perhaps imagine,
    a servant girl,
    the latter two leading an ox.
They came to Bethlehem
    to pay the tribute
    Cæsar had imposed
    on those regions.

Then, set the scene:
    the journey . . .
And then to imagine the cave of the nativity:
    how roomy or how cramped;
    how lofty or how low;
    how is it laid out.

Then contemplate the people there:
    our Lady . . .
    Joseph . . .
    the servant girl . . .
    and, once he is born, the infant.

As if I am really present,
  I place myself in the scene
  as a very poor person,
  not deserving to be there.

I watch them.
I serve them in all their needs,
  with all possible devotion.
I listen to whatever they may be saying,
  and wonder at that as well.

Then I look at what they are doing,
  I take in what is really happening:
  how they journey and toil
  so that the Lord may be born
  in the utmost poverty;
  how, after labours, hunger and thirst,
  after insults and injuries,
  he dies at last on the cross;
  and all of this for my sake.
Then I try to take that to heart.

The Spiritual Exercises, *111-116*

MAY GOD COME AND REIGN (1)

... the reign of truth and of life;
the reign of holiness and grace;
the reign of justice, love and peace.

From the Preface of Christ the King, **Roman Missal**

MAY GOD COME AND REIGN (2)

God is love *(1 John 4:16),*
  and
love is patient and kind
  (1 Corinthians 13:4-8);
  so
God is patient and kind
God is not boastful or arrogant or rude
God is not envious
God does not insist on his own way
God is not irritable or resentful
God does not rejoice in wrongdoing,
  but rejoices in truth
God bears all things
God hopes all things
God endures all things
God who is love never ends.

MAY GOD COME AND REIGN (3)

*The following ancient prayer now appears in our modern **Roman Missal** as the Opening Prayer for the 26th Sunday in Ordinary Time. The version below is a free translation from the Latin that Ignatius would have known and used in his time.*

> God,
>> you show your complete power
>> more than in any other way
>> by showing pity and forgiving;
>> keep pouring your strengthening love
>>> over us
>> so that we may continue pressing forward
>> toward what you promise
>> and so share in the gifts that last for ever.

The Roman Missal

PRESUME GOOD WILL (1)

Both the person
    directing the *Spiritual Exercises*
    and the person making them
    will greatly help and profit each other
    if they take it as read
    that a good Christian
    should be more ready
    to put a good meaning
    on what the other says,
    rather than to condemn it out of hand.

The Spiritual Exercises, *22*

PRESUME GOOD WILL (2)

If you could see into my heart,
    you would all find yourselves there,
    though perhaps you might fail
    to recognise yourselves there,
    so high is the opinion
    I have formed of you.

*Saint Francis Xavier S.J.,
writing from the Far East
to his Companions in Europe*

PRESUME GOOD WILL (3)

Any Gospel scene can be prayed
in the same way
as the example of the Nativity (see pages 32, 33).

Ignatius invites us

· to remember

· to set the scene

· to contemplate the people involved

· to place myself in the scene, with the people

· to watch them, to listen to them.

As we identify, for instance,
with Zacchæus *(Luke 19:1-10)*,
or the Good Thief
(Luke 23:32 . . . 43, especially 39-42),
or the woman
who washes Jesus' feet
with her tears *(Luke 7:36-50)*
or the woman at the well *(John 4:1-42)*
we find that:

1. Jesus treats us kindly,
without asking any questions.

2. We come away more inclined
to give others the benefit of the doubt.

*Based on **The Spiritual Exercises**, 261-312*

To Love . . . and to Follow (1)

Wherever you go, I will go;
    wherever you live, I will live.
Your people shall be my people,
    and your God shall be my God.
Where you die, I will die;
    and there I will be buried.
Heaven forbid it
    that even death should part me from you!

The Song of Ruth (Ruth 1:16-17)

To Love . . . and to Follow (2)

Thanks be to thee, my Lord Jesus Christ,
    for all the benefits thou hast given me,
    for all the pains and insults
    which thou hast borne for me,
    O most merciful Redeemer, Friend and
      Brother.
May I know thee more clearly,
    love thee more dearly
    and follow thee more nearly.

Saint Richard of Chichester (1197-1253)

To Love . . . and to Follow (3)

Here I ask for what I desire:
> I ask for an intimate knowledge of our
>   Lord
> who has entered the human race for me,
> that I may love him more
> and follow him more closely.

The Spiritual Exercises, *104*

INSCAPE AND OUTREACH (1)

What does it mean to be a Jesuit? A Jesuit is one who acknowledges that he is a sinner and yet at the same time called to be a companion of Jesus in the way that Ignatius was once called when he prayed to the Blessed Virgin to set him alongside her Son; he felt that the Father was asking Jesus, in the carrying of his cross, to acknowledge the 'poor pilgrim' as his companion.

But what does it mean to be a companion of Jesus today? It means to engage in the spiritual combat proper to our time under the standard of the cross. The crucial struggle today is being waged on the field of faith and of the justice integral to it.

The Society of Jesus, having come together in the 32nd General Congregation, considers afresh the end for which it was founded: 'the greater glory of God and the service of humanity'. First it confesses with sorrow its sinful failures in maintaining the faith and promoting God's justice. It asks itself again, in the presence of Christ hanging on the cross, 'What have I done for him? what am I doing? what shall I do?', and it judges that Jesuit identity and authentic Jesuit action is determined by the measure of involvement in this combat.

32nd General Congregation of the Society of Jesus, Decree 2 (1975)

INSCAPE AND OUTREACH (2)

The Sisters the Faithful Companions of Jesus
 thirst with Jesus for justice,
 walking gently in solidarity
 with marginalised people
 and with suffering humanity.

The Faithful Companions of Jesus
Extract from their 1997 calendar

INSCAPE AND OUTREACH (3)

Fervour does not consist in feelings,
 nor in pious narcissism,
 but in the will to do good.
It is not the taking of vows,
 nor the approval of superiors
 that gives security,
 but simply and solely
 the search for truth,
 and that is the search for God.

Mary Ward (1585-1645)
Foundress of the Institute of the Blessed Virgin Mary

DECIDING THE BEST WAY FORWARD (1)

For people of good will,
    the good spirit touches their hearts quietly,
    gently and sweetly,
    like a drop of water
    being absorbed by a sponge;
    whereas the evil spirit
    touches their hearts sharply,
    with noise and disquiet,
    like a drop of water falling on a rock.
Like enters like with ease,
    whereas opposites resist one another.

The Spiritual Exercises 335 *(Simple version)*

DECIDING THE BEST WAY FORWARD (2)

I am in your hand:
    turn me this way,
    turn me that way,
    turn me right round in a circle.
Look,
    here I am,
    your servant,
    ready for anything.

Thomas à Kempis
The Imitation of Christ *(Book 3, chapter 15)*

DECIDING THE BEST WAY FORWARD (3)

We can't do it all,
   and we can't do it alone.

There were twelve apostles
   and even they could not do it all,
   even with Jesus amongst them.

They could not do everything,
   but by prayer
   they were able to discern
   their own special apostolate
   using the uniqueness of their own gifts.

Like the first apostles
   we are being called and chosen
   to 'go' and 'do'.

We have indeed been sent –
   sent to where we are,
   to pass on to others
   what we learn from Jesus.

Rita MacManus
Christian Life Community Newsletter
(March 1997)

CONDITIONS OF EMPLOYMENT (1)

(Jesus says to us)
'My will is to bring under my rule
    the whole world of those
    who do not believe (in God's goodness).

So whoever wishes to come with me
    must be content
    with the same daily fare that I use,
    the same drink and clothing,
    and all the rest the same.

Similarly,
    they will have to
    work by day
    and watch by night
    along with me.

Then they will become sharers
    with me in the victory,
    as they have shared
    in the toil and labour.'

The Spiritual Exercises, *93, 95*

CONDITIONS OF EMPLOYMENT (2)

*In Shakespeare's **Henry V**, the King, disguised in ordinary clothes, speaks to some of his soldiers on the eve of the Battle of Agincourt:*

'For, though I speak it to you, I think the king is
    but a man, as I am:
the violet smells to him as it doth to me;
the element shows to him as it doth to me;
all his senses have but human conditions:
his ceremonies laid by, in his nakedness he appears
    but a man;
and though his affections are higher mounted
    than ours,
yet when they stoop, they stoop with the like wing.
Therefore when he sees reason of fears, as we do,
his fears, out of doubt, be of the same relish as
    ours are:
yet in reason, no man should possess him with any
    appearance of fear,
lest he, by showing it, should dishearten his army.'

William Shakespeare (1564-1616)
***Henry V**, act IV, scene 1*

THE HUMAN FAMILY

One by one, Lord,
    I contemplate them
    and I love them,
    all those people that you have given me
    to help and support me.

One by one,
    I count
    the members of that other
    very dear family
    which has come together round about me,
    sharing the same heartfelt affinities as me
    for scientific research and thinking.

Less clearly,
    and without knowing them all,
    but without missing out a single one,
    I evoke all those who together
    form the anonymous, uncountable mass
    of all who live;
    those who come,
    and those who go;
    but especially those who,
    in the truth or through error,
    at their office desk,
    in their laboratory,

or in their factory,
believe in the progress of things
and who continue to pursue
with passion
the light.

From 'Messe sur le monde'
by Pierre Teilhard de Chardin S.J.

A HEROIC PRAYER

I imagine myself in prison with Jesus at night, after the trial by the Sanhedrin and awaiting the trial before Pilate. The two of us are together. I wish I could say to him:

> I would rather
>> be here with you
>> than anywhere else
>> without you.

> I would rather
>> have nothing
>> and be with you
>> than have everything else
>> without you.

> I would rather
>> be mocked and ridiculed
>> with you
>> than be living comfortably
>> and well thought of
>> but without you.

> I would rather
>> hold to your truth
>> and take the consequences
>> than live an easy lie.

I would rather
> have you for my King,
> crown of thorns and all,
> than follow any other leader.
Remember me.

*Based on **The Spiritual Exercises**,*
292, 167, 157, 214

Place Me with Your Son

Simon of Cyrene had to be forced at first, but he must have joined the community later, since his sons are clearly known to Mark and his readers.

And they led him out to crucify him.

And they pressed into service a passer-by, one Simon of Cyrene who was coming in from the country, the father of Alexander and Rufus, to take his cross.

Mark 15:20b-21

All Will Be Well in the End

Thinking of calling fire to earth,
thinking of cold and lonely births,
I'm thinking of pain, thinking of peace,
broken people, songs of grief.
I'm thinking of trapped and twisted lives,
forgotten faces long before they died:
I've seen it all before,
so many voices longing to be told

that all will be well for them
in the end, all will be well
in the end.

Poverty plans and welfare words
empty omens in the air
to haunt the poor, the little ones
with broken hearts and broken homes;
I've heard songs of hate and harsh belief,
songs of anger, so many songs
of grief, of grief,
but all they long for, all they seek
Is not in the fire that burns across the sky,
not in the storm on the scatterstone
    mountain side;
not in the harsh lies, the earthquake scars,
not in the curse of endless wars

but the still, small voice of a silent flame,
waiting in darkness, waiting to be named:
and guarding our hearts with our mantles
we waited at the entrance of the cave . . .

Hoping all will be well, all will be well in
the end.
Hoping all will be well and all will be well
in the end.
And all will be well for them in the end
all will be well, all manner of things for them
and for us will be well in the end,
All will be well
in the end.

Tom McGuinness S.J.

Trust in Providence (1)

Pray
    as if everything
    depended on you;
act
    as though everything
    depends on God.

Saying attributed to Ignatius of Loyola

Trust in Providence (2)

I am not eager, bold
Or strong – all that is past.
I am ready not to do,
At last, at last!

Attributed to
Peter Canisius S.J. (1521-1597)

The Seven Last Words

Contemplating the mysteries
    that took place on the cross,
    recall first
    how Jesus spoke seven words
    on the cross:

he prayed
    for those who were crucifying him;

he gave pardon
    to the thief;

he commended
    Saint John to his Mother
    and his Mother to Saint John;

he said in a loud voice,
    'I am thirsty!',
    and they gave him
    gall and vinegar;

he said
    that he was desolate;

he said
    'The work is completed!';

he said
    'Father,
    I commend my life
    into your hands.'

The Spiritual Exercises, *297*

AFTER THE RESURRECTION

This prayer will be
    for the grace to rejoice
    and be intensely glad
    over such great glory and joy
    of Christ our Lord.

Consider how the divinity
    which seemed to hide itself
    during the Passion
    appears and makes itself known
    so wondrously
    in the most holy Resurrection
    through its most holy effects.

Consider, too,
    the office of Consoler
    which Christ our Lord exercises:
    compare this with the ways
    in which friends usually
    console one another.

First he appeared to the Virgin Mary;
    although this is not said in Scripture
    it does say that he appeared to others.
Surely Scripture supposes
    we have some sense, since it is written:
    'Are you also without understanding?'

Imagine the house
　　where our Lady was staying,
　　and imagine you are there with her . . .
　　imagine the rooms,
　　her own room,
　　the oratory, and so on.
Who is there in this scene?
What are they saying?
What are they doing?

Draw comfort for yourself,
　　and inspiration.

　　　　The Spiritual Exercises,
　　　　221, 223, 224, 220, 299

PERSONALLY LOVED (1)

My Father,
  may your name be revered.
  May your kingdom come.
  Give us each day our daily bread;
  and forgive us our sins,
  since we ourselves let off
    those who are in debt to us.
  And please do not lead us into any test.

The Lord's Prayer according to Luke 11:2-4

PERSONALLY LOVED (2)

Thanks to Jesus, we can take the loving words of
Scripture for ourselves:

'This is the Word of the Lord

    about ....

Do not fear, ...
    for I have redeemed you;

I have called you, ... ,
    by name, you are mine.'   *(see Isaiah 43:1)*

'But you said,
    "The Lord has forsaken me,
    my Lord has forgotten me!"

Can a woman forget the child she is nursing,
or show no compassion for the child of her womb?

Even these may forget,
    but I will never forget ....

See, I have inscribed you
on the palm of my hands.'   *(see Isaiah 49:14-16)*

'It was I who taught you to walk,
I took you up in my arms.'   *(see Hosea 11:3)*

Brian Grogan S.J.

Prayer of an Ageing Jesuit

This prayer first appeared in the May 1973 News-letter of the Venice-Milan Province of the Jesuits. It has since been translated and widely reprinted.

Dearest Lord, teach me to grow old gracefully.
Help me to see that my community does me no
    wrong
when gradually it takes me from my duties;
when it no longer seems to seek my views.

Rid me of my pride in all the 'wisdom' I have
    learned.
Rid me of the illusion that I am indispensable.

Help me in this gradual detachment from earthly
    things
to grasp the meaning of your law of time.

Teach me, in this turn-over of work and workers,
to discern a striking expression of life's constant
    renewal
under the impulse of your providence.

And please, Lord, let me still be useful,
contributing to the world with my optimism,
adding my prayers to the joyful fervour and
    courage
of those who now take their turn at the helm.

Let my life-style now become one of humble and
    serene
contact with the world in change,
shedding no tears for the past;
making of my human sufferings
a gift of reparation to all my brothers.

Let my leaving the field of action be simple and
    natural –
like a glowing, cheerful sunset.

Lord, forgive me if only now in my tranquillity
I begin to know how much you love me,
how much you've helped me.

And now, finally,
may I have a clear, a deep understanding
of the joyful destiny you have prepared for me
guiding my every step from the first day of my
    life.

Lord, teach me to grow old . . . just so.

FINDING GOD IN ALL THINGS

Think how many gifts God has given me,
    gifts of
        nature
        salvation
        gifts personal to me.
Take time about it;
    count them up.
God never says so,
    but shouldn't I offer matching gifts
        to God?

Think how the great God
    seems to want to live in me
    in a way more personal
    than the way he lives in metals,
        plants,
        or animals,
    almost making of me
    a temple of God.
Should I not want to return the visit,
    and indeed stay there with God?

Think how God has been at work
    for me and for mine
    since the beginning of time.
Should I not want to do some work for God?

As the sun is in the sunbeam,
 as the river is in every droplet,
 so God is in everything
 and in every moment.
God, may I find you there
 and keep you.

How can I pay you back
 for the two eyes with which I am blessed?
Where would I find another pair to give,
 and how could I ever afford them . . .
 just one gift out of thousands?
Instead, I give to you
 the pair you gave me,
 I give them
 for your use and your service.

The Spiritual Exercises, *231-237*

Take and Receive

Jesus,
    I give you my hands to work with,
    my eyes to see with.
If there is anyone you wish to speak to,
    use my feet to get there,
    and then my tongue
    to speak with them.
If you wish to listen to anyone,
    use my ears.
I give you my permission,
    any time you wish.
I give you
    my memory
        to remember with,
    my mind
        to think with,
    my heart
        to love with.
You have many other ways
    of reaching your sisters and brothers
    but if you ever wish to use me
    as your messenger,
    I would be honoured indeed.
You have my permission.

The Spiritual Exercises, 234

ALL I NEED

First,
> love is to be found
> in deeds
> rather than in words.

Great God,
> give me only your love
>> (to know you love me)
> and your grace
>> (the strength to love you back).

These are enough for me,
> and I ask nothing more.

Amen.

The Spiritual Exercises, *230, 234*